Tzitzit

You shall make yourself tassels on the four corners of the garment

Tzitzit

YOU SHALL MAKE YOURSELF TASSELS ON
THE FOUR CORNERS OF THE GARMENT

By Toby Janicki

FIRST FRUITS OF
ZION

First Fruits of Zion is a 501(c)(3) registered nonprofit educational organization.

First Edition 2011
Printed in the United States of America

ISBN: 978-1-892124-62-3

Unless otherwise noted, Scripture quotations are taken from the New American Standard Bible®, Copyright © 1960, 1962, 1963, 1968, 1971, 1972, 1973, 1975, 1977, 1995 by The Lockman Foundation. Used by permission (www.Lockman.org). The author substituted "Messiah" for "Christ" and "Yeshua" for "Jesus" with permission from The Lockman Foundation.

Cover Design: Avner Wolff
Cover Photograph: © iStockphoto/Patrick Banks

Quantity discounts are available on bulk purchases of this book for educational, fundraising or event purposes. Special versions or book excerpts to fit specific needs are available from First Fruits of Zion. For more information, contact www.ffoz.org/contact.

First Fruits of Zion

PO Box 649, Marshfield, Missouri 65706–0649 USA
Phone (417) 468–2741, www.ffoz.org

Comments and questions: www.ffoz.org/contact

Thus says HaShem, Master of Legions:
"In those days a minyan from the nations
of every language shall take hold of
the tzitzit of Mashiach, saying,
'Let us go with you, for we have heard
that God is with you.'"

(Zechariah 8:23)

Contents

Introduction

There once lived a woman who suffered from hemorrhaging for twelve years.[1] She had exhausted all of her money on doctors, but their remedies provided her no relief or improvement. Instead, her ailment only grew worse and worse. For twelve years she had been isolated from her beloved husband. For twelve years she was not able to go to the holy Temple in Jerusalem to offer up petitions to God in the holiest place on earth. For twelve years her Passover was diminished; her condition prohibited her from eating of the Pesach lamb. She began to lose all hope that life would ever be normal again. She had already given up on doctors, healers, cures, and medicines, and she felt like giving up on her heavenly Father as well.

One day she began to hear reports about a certain charismatic rabbi named Yeshua ben Yosef from Capernaum who had healing powers. All her friends and family began urging her, "Go to Capernaum and see Rabbi Yeshua." At first she dismissed it as a false hope, but between everyone's persistence and the ever-increasing number of miraculous stories about the rabbi, she was finally persuaded to go out and to seek him.

When she arrived at the docks of Capernaum early the next morning, a huge crowd had already gathered to wait for Rabbi Yeshua's boat to arrive. When his boat finally docked, the crowd pressed in so thickly that she could not even see his face. She thought to herself, "Perhaps, just perhaps, he is *the* Prophet that Israel has been waiting for."

She noticed that he was hurrying off with the important head of the Capernaum synagogue. She sighed, "He has no time for me." But then a thought occurred to her, "If I can only touch the *tzitzit* ("fringe") of his cloak, I will be healed."

1

She pushed her way into the midst of the jostling crowd, following him until she was right behind him. Stooping low, as if to pick something up, she unobtrusively took hold of one of the tzitzit that hung from the four corners of his cloak. She only touched it for a brief moment, but immediately she could feel a rush of warmth flow through her body, and she knew beyond a shadow of a doubt that she had been healed. She quickly released the tzitzit and attempted to move away unnoticed.

But Rabbi Yeshua sensed that something special had just happened. The instant that the woman felt the flow of the Holy Spirit into her body, he also felt the power of the Spirit flow out of him. Rabbi Yeshua turned to the crowd and asked, "Who touched my garments?" Instantly, fear came over the woman.

The question puzzled the disciples. They pointed out that the crowd thronged about him on every side and that many people were bumping against him. The people around him denied having touched him. One of Rabbi Yeshua's disciples responded, "Master, the people are crowding and pressing in on you!"

Yet, the rabbi persisted, "Someone did *intentionally* touch me. I felt the power go out of me."

The frightened woman saw that she had not escaped notice. Fearful and trembling, she stepped forward from the crowd. She prostrated herself before Rabbi Yeshua and confessed the whole story like a guilty child confessing a theft. She knew that she had committed an impropriety. In her state of ritual contamination, she should not have been touching people and transmitting ritual impurity.

She winced as she waited for a rebuke. Instead, the Rabbi Yeshua smiled from ear to ear and with great joy said "Daughter, your faith has made you well; go in shalom, and be healed of your disease."

This story from the Gospels is timeless. It is told over and over—the simple faith with which people may approach the Master and the love that our Messiah has for his people. Less examined is the question of why the woman assumed that simply grasping the Master's tzitzit would heal her? She was not the only one. Many others did the same thing in hopes of being healed from their ailments as well.[2] In fact, the prophet Zechariah tells us that in the end of days many from the nations who wish to join themselves to Messiah will grasp a hold of his tzitzit.[3] There is deep meaning to these actions, and we miss a great deal of the significance of these scriptural passages when we don't know the background.

In this book, with God's help, I will attempt to unravel the mystery of the tzitzit. It is my desire to educate both Jews and Christians about the function and symbolism of the tzitzit. While this is not an exhaustive study, I pray it will serve as a useful introduction to the subject.

1
Torah Commandment

If you are an observant Jew, you might be very familiar with tzitzit—the dangly strings that hang from the four corners of one's prayer shawl or *tallit katan*. Even if you are not familiar with tzitzit, you may have seen them before, hanging off the hips of orthodox Jewish men, like four long strands of knotted threads. They are usually white and hang from the belt level to about the knees, bobbing around as one walks.

Man wearing tzitzit in Israel.

For westerners, such archaic garb seems superfluous. At best it could be viewed as a quaint, albeit impractical, relic from the past. We might ask ourselves what could be the purpose of these long, dangly strings? Does God really want his people wearing them? Is this really a biblical commandment?

Believe it or not, God commands the Jewish people to wear tassels in two separate places in the Torah:

> The LORD said to Moses, "Speak to the people of Israel, and tell them to make tassels (tzitzit, ציצת) on the corners of their garments throughout their generations, and to put a cord of blue on the tassel (tzitzit, ציצת) of each corner. And it shall be a tassel (tzitzit, ציצת) for you to look at and remember all the commandments of the LORD, to do them, not to follow after your own heart and your own eyes, which you are inclined to whore after. So you shall remember and do all my commandments, and be holy to your God. I am the LORD your God, who brought you out of the land of Egypt to be your God: I am the LORD your God." (Numbers 15:37–41)

> You shall make yourself tassels) *gedilim*, גדלים) on the four corners of the garment with which you cover yourself. (Deuteronomy 22:12)

Jewish tradition teaches that both of these passages are about the single commandment of attaching tassels to the four corners of one's garments and placing a thread of blue among the threads of those fringes.[4] According to Maimonides' list of the 613 commandments of the Torah, this is positive commandment number sixteen.[5] The Numbers passage tells us that the purpose of the tassels is to look upon them and remember the commandments of the Torah and in turn do them.

In Numbers the word *tzitzit* (ציצת) means "tassel"; it can also be used in the sense of a "lock" of hair, as in Ezekiel 8:3.[6] Deuteronomy employs the word *gedilim* (גדלים), which means "twists" or "braids of thread."[7] First Kings 7:17 uses the word *gedilim* to describe "wreaths of chain work for the capitals on the tops of the pillars." To reconcile these two terms, ancient Jewish tradition viewed *gedilim* as referring to the top knotted section of the tassel and *tzitzit* as the loose strings that hang off the bottom end.[8] While both definitions are satisfied by the actual traditional Jewish practice, these tassels are primarily known as tzitzit. The word tzitzit is technically singular, referring to one tassel. The plural of tzitzit in Hebrew is *tzitziyot*. However, in English people commonly use the singular form tzitzit for both singular and plural.

Unlike other Torah practices such as tefillin and mezuzah, tzitzit have been interpreted as being a literal commandment universally by all sects of Judaism.

2

Cultural Background

Even if it is in the Bible, the idea of wearing long strings still seems kind of weird. Why would God command the Jewish people to wear strings? Does he have an affection for tassels? Actually, it makes a lot more sense when we examine the culture of the Ancient Near East. The wearing of tassels is not a practice that began with the Israelites, nor is it unique to the Bible. It was actually a phenomenon that existed pre-Sinai, before the Torah was given, and was a style of dress worn by many different cultures. Therefore, in context, it is actually not strange at all but fits right in with the fashions of the Ancient Near East.

We find many examples from wall paintings and stone carvings of clothing with tassels attached to them. The hem was usually the most ornate part of one's garment. The more wealthy and important the individual, the more ornate the hem of his garment.[9] It was a sign of power, authority, and kingship.[10] The tassel was considered an extension of that hem. For example in one wall painting in Thebes, Egypt, dating to the 15th century BCE, we find a color picture of tassels with red and blue threads in them.[11]

Because of the importance of both the hem and the tassel, it was a sign of disgrace in the Ancient Near East to have them torn off.[12] Jacob Milgrom writes:

> In Mesopotamia we find early Akkadian texts (for example, in 18th-century Mari) which frequently use the phrase "to cut off the hem" (*sisikta bataqu*). When the hem is cut off, a part of the person's personality is removed.[13]

That cultural context explains David's remorse for cutting off the hem of Saul's garment.

And afterward David's heart struck him, because he had cut off a corner of Saul's robe. He said to his men, "The LORD forbid that I should do this thing to my lord, the LORD's anointed, to put out my hand against him, seeing he is the LORD's anointed." (1 Samuel 24:5–7)

One midrash illustrates the gravity of David's offense: "What is the difference between cutting off the tzitzit and cutting off the head?" (*Midrash Tehillim* 7:5).[14]

Another cultural custom was to grab the hem of another person's garment in situations where one was attempting to persuade that person to grant a favor. This is illustrated in 1 Samuel 15 where Saul seizes the hem of the prophet Samuel's garment in a last-ditch effort to get him to intercede on his behalf. It's the "old custom of seizing the [hem] as a means of bringing added pressure to bear upon the will of the person from whom a request was made."[15]

The hem of a man's garment could be used as a legal seal on clay documents. Dignitaries and the upper-class noblemen used the distinctive pattern of threads on their ornate hems as a seal impression. They would press the hem of their garment into the clay documents as a sort of signature.[16] Some suggest that this might be the origin behind the custom of touching of the Torah Scroll with one's tzizit during the synagogue service; the custom may have been originally instituted as a legal gesture, reaffirming the Jewish people's commitment to the Torah.[17] Just as an impression of the hem in clay was a symbol of "surrender to punishment in case of non-compliance,"[18] so the touching of the Torah with one's tzitzit might be a symbol of submission. We even find the practice of oath-taking by grabbing hold of the tzitzit (similar to the modern way one places his hand on the Bible) in an 11th-century midrash:

It has become customary in Israel to tender one's fringe of tzitzit to another for the loan of money. (*Bereshit Rabbati*)[19]

3
History of Application

In most Jewish communities today the commandment of tzitzit is observed in two ways: Jewish men wear a *tallit* ("prayer shawl," טלית, plural: *tallitot*), a four-corned sheet with a tzitzit attached to each corner, during morning prayers. Observant Jewish men also wear a *tallit katan* ("small tallit," טלית קטן), a smaller four-cornered sheet with tzitzit on the corners and a hole in the middle, under their clothes as a sort of undershirt throughout the day. In ancient times the practice was slightly different. Let's examine the development of these customs.

Tallit

Today Jewish men use the *tallit* as a ritual garment—a prayer shawl, but in Bible-times, the *tallit* was not a ritual garment, it was a man's cloak.

At the time when the Torah was given many different people groups, not just the Israelites, wore an outer garment that looked much like a sheet or blanket. This rectangular outer garment, sometimes with a hole for the head, sometimes simply wrapped around the body, had four corners. They were rectangular in shape because they were woven on looms. Such garments became the origin of the tallit in Biblical times. The only religious significance associated with the Israelites' tallit was the tzitzit attached to them. The original tallit was merely an outer garment resembling the common blanket-like garment that men wore.[20] We find an early depiction of this in ancient Israel through an archaeological find. In the mid-nineteenth century, a black limestone relief sculpture from Nimrud in northern Iraq was found that depicts an Israelite king (perhaps Jehu) bowing before the Assyrian king Shalmaneser III (858–824 BCE). The Israelite king is depicted as wearing "a girdle with tas-

11

sels on the end [that] is tied around his middle," while the other Israelites have "a fringed outer garment with tassels on a section thrown over the shoulder."[21]

Black limestone relief sculpture from Nimrud in northern Iraq depicting King Jehu of Israel bowing before Shalmanezer III (858 -824 BCE) of Assyria. With permission from zyworld.com.

We learn further background information in the Gospels where the Master states: "And if anyone would sue you and take your tunic, let him have your cloak as well" (Matthew 5:40).[22] The Greek word here for "tunic," *chiton* (χιτων), corresponds to the rabbinic Hebrew *chaluk* (חלוק), which is a "plain smooth undergarment" usually made of linen.[23] Whereas "cloak," *himation* (ιματιον), would correspond to *tallit* which was a heavier outer garment generally made of wool.[24] The tallit is also the "robe" that the Master was referring to in Mark 12:38 and Luke 20:46. We find depictions of *himation* in paintings from the Dura-Europas synagogue excavated in modern day Syria dating back to the 3rd century CE.[25]

By the first century, it was considered somewhat immodest for Jewish men to be seen in public without wearing a *tallit*, the exception being when performing strenuous labor.[26] The Talmud describes the tallit as worn draped over the shoulder or doubled over like a sheet.[27] It measured about a handbreadth (about 2½ to 4 inches) shorter than the undergarment.[28] Scholars feel that the ancient tallit of

Depiction of a *himation* with fringes from the Dura-Europas synagogue (3rd Century CE).

the first few centuries CE most likely resembled the *bayah* "blanket" still worn by Bedouin today.²⁹ The sages of the late Second Temple period often wore a finer quality tallit that is comparable to the ancient Roman *pallium*.³⁰

Remember though, these *tallitot* were not ritual garments, like prayer shawls that men wore at synagogue. They were the clothing that people wore on their backs every day.

Tallit Katan

After the destruction of the Temple, when much of Israel was forced into exile, the tzitzit became an identity marker for the Jewish people that often brought with it harassment and persecution. Combining this with the changing styles in clothes, some

Roman *pallium* over a *chiton*.

Jewish men chose to give up the practice of the tallit outside of prayer. Rabbi Abraham ibn Ezra (1093–1167) laments:

However I believe that one is more obligated to enwrap oneself in fringes when he is not at prayer than during the time of prayer, so that he remembers the commandments and does not err and trespass during the other hours of the day, for in the hour of prayer he will not will into sin.³¹

To correct this problem, sometime during the Middle Ages, Jewish men almost universally adopted the practice of wearing a *tallit katan* under their clothes. This way the mitzvah of tzitzit could still be observed despite the changing fashions and the rise in persecution.

Did the Master and the apostles wear a *tallit katan*? Probably not. It is difficult to know with any certainty when the *tallit katan* came into vogue. While "there is no explicit mention of the *tallit katan* in the *Talmud* … a story related in b.*Menachot* 44a appears to indicate that such garments were worn in that era."[32] Other than this, the oldest literary record of the *tallit katan* comes from the fourteenth century in Jacob ben Asher's *Tur Orach Chayyim*.[33] Today however, wearing a *tallit katan* is a common practice for observant Jewish men.

An Amazing Discovery

In the spring of 1960, archaeologist Yigael Yadin found a group of documents in a cave that was located in a wadi along the western shore of the Dead Sea. At the time of the discovery, no one guessed its significance. Scholars soon found that among the various names mentioned in these papyri was that of the infamous Shimon bar Kochba. Bar Kochba was the famous Jewish leader who led the unsuccessful revolt against Rome in 135 CE. He was as popular as he was controversial, and to discover a cave in which it seems that his followers had hidden was no less than spectacular. These findings are a great window into the culture and life of the period surrounding the late Second Temple period up to the second century CE. In a series of caves in the area that become known as the Bar Kochba Caves, all kinds of artifacts were found, ranging from clothing to pottery to weapons.

One significant archaeological discovery has actually provided us with examples of *tallitot* worn by Jewish people not long after the days of the apostles. All the *tallitot* that were found were made of wool.[34] Additionally, although they came in various different colors, the designs and patterns were very similar in nature. This included vertical stripes much like those in the tallit of today. Yadin notes that this carryover of patterns illustrates "the force of tradition."[35]

The Fringes

In addition to *tallitot*, the findings at the Bar Kochba caves helped shed some light on the fringes themselves. Although no tzitzit were found on the actual *tallitot* due to the long-standing tradition of cutting the tzitzit off a tallit in which one is buried, two kinds of thread were found from what appears to be unfinished tzitzit. Blue (*techelet*) strands made of wool and white strands made of linen were found together.[36] The linen threads themselves were about 8–9cm long when halved.[37]

The mixing of wool and linen (*sha'atnez*, שעטנז) in garments is expressly forbidden by the Torah.[38] Despite this fact, the rabbis actually ruled that this mixture should be in the tzitzit.[39] As we shall discuss later, this may have been due to rabbinic interpretation surrounding the close proximity of the commandment regarding tzitzit and that of *sha'atnez* in Deuteronomy 22. It might also have been for the practical reason that linen being the whitest of materials would be very appropriate for the white of the tzitzit, but at the same time was unsuitable for *techelet* because it could not be dyed. In that regard, the commandment to place a thread of blue in the tzitzit is actually a commandment to mix wool and linen—an exception to the rule.

TEIMANIM

Before we leave our study of the history of tzitzit it would be worth touching on the practice of the *Teimanim* ["Yeminite Jews," תימנים]. Jewish people have lived in Yemen for over 1800 years. These Jews have been largely isolated from the rest of the Jewish world and overshadowed in their own country by Islam. This unique setting of isolation has caused them to preserve many of the more ancient forms of halachic practice.

> The Jewish community of Yemen was unique in the degree
> to which it preserved its ancient traditions instead of
> absorbing the new customs from Palestine.[40]

Under Islamic rule in Yemen, Jews were subject to dress restrictions which often did not allow them to wear modern clothing.[41] These factors have combined to preserve an earlier form of tzitzit than exists today in other Jewish communities.

Although there were certain periods in Yemenite Jewish history where influences from modern Judaism were stronger than others, it was not until just over a hundred years ago that the *Teimanim* had begun on a large scale to connect with the rest of Judaism as a whole and to adopt many of the more modern practices.[42] Since 1881 almost the entire *Teimanim* population has immigrated to Israel.[43]

When we examine the practice of the tallit and tzitzit that existed in Yemen prior to this integration, we get a glimpse of the older practice of wearing the tallit all day as a regular garment without a *tallit katan*. The leading Yemenite rabbi of his day, Rav Yosef Kafah (1917–2000), describes the tradition of the Yemenite tallit which is called *shamlei* ("my garments") in Arabic:

> On the week days the people came back from the *beit knesset* ["synagogue"] with the *tallitot*. They didn't have a *tallit katan* (per se). Instead, they wore a black fabric (which did have tzitzit) to sit on and protect themselves. It is like a *tallit katan* (but) over the shoulders and it served protective purposes. This was only on the weekdays. This was called the *shamlei*.[44]

Their tallit was a square garment made of thick lamb's wool and was usually black, sometimes containing white stripes. Unlike many of their rabbinic counterparts, they also left the ends of their tallit untrimmed as decoration which they claim is also an older custom.[45] The tallit was worn on the shoulder and, in accordance with the older rabbinic custom, a man would never go out of his house without it. Apparently, as Rabbi Jacob Sapir describes of his visit to Yemen in the 1800s, it was used as well for a variety of tasks:

> They cover themselves with the *shamlei* throughout the day … at night too they cover themselves with it, or use it to cover the mattress on which they lie. And it will be used for every task; people carry things in it when they go buying and selling in the market, or they use it to carry wood.[46]

According to Rav Kafah the tallit was used in contractual agreements as well, which is like the customs already mentioned from the Ancient Near East.[47]

Another peculiarity of the practice of the Yemenites is the way in which they tie their tzitzit. They claim that their practice of seven to thirteen groups of three *chulyot* ["circular wraps," חוליות] with no knots in between is closer to the ancient tradition as found in the Talmud.[48] Rav Kafah states that, "such is our custom from of old,"[49] and Rabbi Isaac Ratsaby adds:

At any rate, it would seem that a clear preference should be given to our custom, which explicitly appears in the Talmud, whereas other practices were introduced without any comparable source. (*Olat Yitzhak*, *Siman* 13)[50]

It appears that many of the customs and practices of the *Teimanim* are indeed ancient and could go back to the Second Temple period and even earlier. However, it should be noted that today, most *Teimanim* now living in Israel have conformed to the modern practice of wearing a tallit only while praying in the morning and a *tallit katan* throughout the day, though they still retain their unique style of tying tzitzit and leaving the ends of their tallit untrimmed. Thus they have found a way to preserve their unique traditions while at the same time integrating into contemporary halachah.

Continuity

For the most part the practice of tzitzit has changed very little over the years. Traditional Judaism has managed to keep current with the styles of dress and of progress with the *tallit katan* while at the same time maintaining the original garment during prayer with the tallit. Observing the commandment in this traditional way can give Jewish men a real sense of continuity and connection with the many generations of Israelites that have worn tzitzit—including our Master himself.

4
The Master and Tzitzit

When we think of the religious practice of our Master we often focus on the emphasis he placed on the moral and ethical commandments of the Torah such as loving your neighbor and caring for the poor. Most believers do not picture Yeshua as particularly observant of the injunctions in the Torah that are more ceremonial or ritual in nature. We usually view him as easily dismissing these as outward trappings and unnecessary legalism. Bringing this mindset into the discussion of this book then, it begs the question, would Yeshua have worn tzitzit? Furthermore, didn't he actually criticize the Pharisees for wearing them? To answer this question, a thorough examination of the pertinent Gospel passages is in order.

In the story of healing of the woman with the issue of blood, we read that she "touched the fringe of his garment" (Matthew 9:20).[51] The word for fringe in Greek is *kraspedon* (κρασπεδον), which is the direct equivalent of tzitzit in the Septuagint. David Bivin suggests rendering the phrase as *tzitziyot talito* ("The *tzitzit* of his *tallit*," ציציות טליתו).[52] This would have distinguished the Master from the *am ha'aretz* (impious, עם הארץ) who did not wear tzitzit.[53]

Translators have often obscured Yeshua wearing tzitzit by their translation bias. This is done by translating the Greek word *kraspedon* one way when it comes to Yeshua (e.g., Matthew 9:20) and another way when it comes to the Pharisees (e.g., Matthew 23:5). For example:[54]

Bible Version	Matthew 9:20	Matthew 23:5
The New Testament in Modern English	"the edge of his cloak"	"the tassels of their robes"
The Message	"his robe"	"embroidered prayer shawls"
Good News Bible	"the edge of his cloak"	"tassels on their robes"

Unfortunately, this maintains the stereotype of the "hypo-critical" Pharisees wearing tzitzit while the non-Torah-observant Yeshua only wears a robe with a big blue, purple, or red sash.

Instead, the Greek clearly indicates that both Yeshua and the Pharisees wore tzitzit.

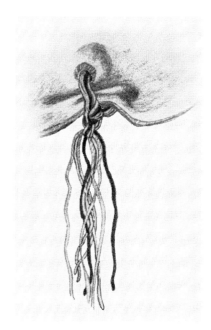

Reconstruction drawing of a first century tzitzit. Helen Twena, Jerusalem Perspective ©1999. Used with permission.

YESHUA'S TASSELS

Based upon our review above of the history of tzitzit, the Master's tzitzit would have been attached to a four cornered blanket-like sheet that he would have worn throughout the day except in the house or during strenuous labor. He would have worn this over his linen tunic-like garment (*chaluk*). His tallit would have most likely been made of wool, possibly even with stripes running along two of the ends. The Master would have worn this either over his shoulder or doubled over like a sheet.[55] It is also possible, based on the expensive seamless under-tunic he wore (John 19:23), that the Master owned a finer quilt style of tallit that the scholars and sages wore.

According to some scholars, there is also evidence that, already by the Master's time, it was a widespread tradition to pull the tallit over one's head during prayer.[56] In fact Yadin believes that the stripes present on the upper edges of the tallitot found at the Bar Kochba caves could have been for framing the face when it was pulled over the head for prayer.[57] It is likely that the Master adhered to this custom.

The healing of a bleeding woman from the Catacombs of Marcellinus and Peter in Rome (4th Century).

GRASPING THE FRINGES

In our introduction we told the story of a woman who seeks healing by grasping hold of the Master's tzitzit. It may be that the woman was somehow trying to get God's attention by doing this. Yet there is more than just Near Eastern culture involved here. It was believed in the days of the Master that the tzitzit of *chasidim* ("pious ones") could bring miracles.[58] Note this story from the Talmud:

> Channan the Hidden was the son of the daughter of Choni the Circle-Drawer. When the world was in need of rain the rabbis would send to him school children and they would take hold of the hem of his garment and say to him, "Abba, Abba, give us rain." Thereupon he would plead with the Holy One, Blessed be He, "Master of the Universe, do it for the sake of these who are unable to distinguish between the Father who gives rain and the father who does not." (b. *Ta'anit* 23b)[59]

In the Gospel story the woman did not need to get the attention of Yeshua; instead, she believed that just by touching his tzitzit she would be healed. Her faith brought her a miracle from HaShem.

Consider the words of the prophet Malachi when he says, "the sun of righteousness will rise with healing in its wings." (Malachi 4:2 [3:20]). In Biblical Hebrew the word for wing (*kanaf*, כנף) is identical to the word for corner. Numbers 15 mandates tying *tzitzit* onto the corners/wings of the garment. Armed with confidence that this Yeshua from Nazareth must be the prophesied "sun of righteousness," the woman felt certain that if only she could lay hold of his wings (that is the corners of his garments to which the *tzitzit* were attached) she would surely be healed of her affliction.

Lengthening Tassels

The Master also offered some criticism of the way some of the religious fashion moguls of his day carried out this commandment in an ostentatious manner.

> They do all their deeds to be seen by others. For they make their phylacteries broad and their fringes [tzitzit] long. (Matthew 23:5)[60]

In this passage Yeshua offered up a halachic ruling about how the tzitzit should be worn. The sages of that day ruled that there was no fixed length for the tzitzit.[61] But it appears that "those of the strict observance—or who pretended to be, as Jesus complained—

favored long tassels."[62] Yeshua saw that some had turned tzitzit into a show of piety in order to appear righteous in the sight of man. It's not the wearing of tzitzit that he criticized but rather the lengthening of them for show which he opposed.

There is a story in the Talmud of a man named *Ben Tzitzit* ("son of tzitzit") who was so wealthy that he had cushions laid out before him so that his tzitzit would not drag on the ground.[63] Some have used this story as an example of someone who had extra long tzitzit, but it must be remembered that the tallit of those days extended well below the knees so that for the tzitzit to touch the ground they would not have to be very long.[64] The point of the story is to emphasize how wealthy *Ben Tzitzit* was and not to point out that he had long tzitzit.

In conclusion, we can see that the Master was as faithful to the commandment of tzitzit as he was to the rest of the Torah. He wore tzitzit in fulfillment of Numbers 15. He taught his disciples to observe this mitzvah discreetly, not as an ostentatious, attention-grabbing demonstration of piety.

5

Symbolism

REMEMBERING

> And it shall be a tassel for you to look at and remember all the commandments of the LORD, to do them, not to follow after your own heart and your own eyes, which you are inclined to whore after. (Numbers 15:39)

One of the most basic purposes of the tzitzit is that they are to serve as a reminder of the commandments of the Torah. The word for "remember" in Numbers 15:39 is the Hebrew word *zachar* (זכר) which means "to be mindful, to pay heed, signifying a sharp focus of attention upon someone or something … and is active not passive … so that it leads to action."[65] This is best summarized in the rabbinic saying, "looking [upon it] leads to remembering, and remembering leads to doing [the commandments]."[66] In Hebrew thought you have not truly remembered something if it does not lead to action.

Jewish scholar Jacob Milgrom argues that the word "tzitzit" could possibly be rendered "something to look at."[67] In that case the name for the tzitzit itself beckons us to look at them.

How do strings and knots serve as a reminder of God's commandments? Biblical scholar Solomon Gandz finds examples of knots and strings being used as mnemonic devices in various cultures. For example, he describes the use of the *khipu* among the ancient Incans:

> A main cord held horizontally, to which were fastened at given distances other cords of various colors and lengths vertically. The vertical cords were knotted in different ways, all these knots of different sizes and shapes and the

various lengths and colors of cords served by means of an arranged code to convey certain numbers, words, phrases, and ideas.[68]

Therefore this might be similar to the modern idea of tying a string around one's finger, but it seems that this Torah commandment reaches to an even deeper level.

One clue might be found in the single blue thread that is woven into the tzitzit. Numbers 15:38 calls for a thread of blue on each of the four corners, but not just any shade of blue will do. The Torah uses the word *techelet* (תכלת), a very specific type of blue dye. There is debate about the source of ancient *techelet*-dye. We will explore those issues in the next chapter. Although some rabbis disagree about the source of the blue dye, everyone agrees that the color was symbolic of the heavenly realms:

> Rabbi Meir used to say, "Why is *techelet* specified from all the other colors? Because blue resembles the color of the sea, and the sea resembles the color of the sky, and the sky resembles the color of [a sapphire, and a sapphire resembles the color of] the Throne of Glory, as it is said, 'And there was under his feet as it were a paved work of sapphire stone'(Ezekiel 24:10), and it is also written, 'The likeness of a throne as the appearance of a sapphire stone' (Ezekiel 1:26)." (b.*Menachot* 43b)

The mystics teach that the color of *techelet* reminds us of HaShem on his throne. The color blue causes the Jewish man to think about who is ultimately the king, i.e., HaShem himself. Thus, the Jew, as a member of God's kingdom, should desire to do God's will as it is expressed in the *mitzvot*. The *techelet* reminds Israel to "climb numerous steps along [their] spiritual path … many of those steps [they] must reclimb after having fallen from previous heights."[69]

An anomaly in the text that cannot be seen in English translations hints at further meaning. In Numbers 15:39 (often translated as "you shall look upon them,") "them" (*oto*, אתו) is in the masculine singular form whereas we would expect it to be in the feminine plural based on the fact that the word *tzitzit* is feminine. Rabbi Meir suggests that *oto* here refers to HaShem himself:

> It is not written, "and you shall see *them*" [the tzitzit], but "you shall see *him*"; which suggests that to him who keeps this commandment it is reckoned as though he had received the face of the Shechinah. (*Sifre* 115)[70]

The Shechinah (שכינה) is God's manifest presence here on earth. Thus the thread of *techelet* is a reminder not only of God on his throne but of his dwelling presence on earth. Not only is he above in the heavenly realms but he is also dwelling here among us. Looking upon the tzitzit should bring feelings of awe and reverence for the Creator. The Baal Shem Tov wrote:

> When donning the *talit* one is to see the "blue thread." This means that awe come upon him. (*Tzava'at Harivash* 21)[71]

The sages connect looking at the tzitzit with looking at the bronze serpent: "With the *tzitzit*, as with the brass snake, 'every one that is bitten, when he sees it he shall live.'"[72]

Because of these concepts of looking, remembering and doing, Rebbe Schneerson taught that the tzitzit are symbolic of our very connection to HaShem.

> The motif of the mitzvah of *tzitzis* is—utter dedication to God which is rooted in the very essence of the soul. Therefore, the Torah mentions not only that you will, "remember all the commandments of God" (Numbers 15:39), but furthermore, you will remember and perform all, "*My* commandments" (verse 40), indicating a bond to the very essence of God. (*Likutei Sichos* 36:160)[73]

Observing God's commandments allows the Israelite to tap into his very will and essence. Therefore the tzitzit, which is a reminder of those commandments, are a representation of Israel's bond to the very core of who HaShem is.

The Episode of the Spies

> And it shall be a tassel for you to look at and remember all the commandments of the LORD, to do them, not to follow after your own heart and your own eyes, which you are inclined to whore after. (Numbers 15:39)

We can gain a further understanding of the tzitzit when we examine the context in which this commandment is given in Numbers 15. This mitzvah is given right after the spies have returned from the land of Israel with an evil report and the Exodus generation is punished by being doomed to die in the wilderness. Remarkably the text of the Torah uses some of the same language in the giving of the commandment of the tzitzit as in the episode of the spies:

Episode of the Spies	Commandment of Tzitzit
Send men to **spy** (*tur*, תור) out the land of Canaan. (Numbers 13:2)	And it shall be a tassel for you to look at and remember all the commandments of the LORD, to do them, not to **follow** (*tur*, תור) after your own heart and your own eyes, which you are inclined to **whore** (*zanah*, זנה) after. (Numbers 15:39)
At the end of forty days they returned from **spying out** (*tur*, תור) the land. (Numbers 13:25)	
According to the number of the days in which you **spied out** (*tur*, תור) the land. (Numbers 14:34)	
And your children shall be shepherds in the wilderness forty years and shall suffer for your **faithlessness** (*zenut*, זנות). (Numbers 14:33)	

Thus the tzitzit are reminders of the danger of what happens when we rely on our own heart and eyes and not on our Father in Heaven and his precious Torah. According to Rabbi Hirsch the word *tur* implies here "an effort to get to know things as to how they can be of use and help to us."[74] Essentially when we rely on our heart and on our eyes in "spying out" what is good and what is not, we end up designating things as good based on our own "sensuous nature" and bad because they do not satisfy our appetite. This is what happened with the spies. They relied on their own observations and did not look through the lens of God's word.

The Talmud elaborates further on the meaning of each sin in Numbers 15:

> "After your own heart:" this refers to heresy; and so it says, "The fool hath said in his heart, "There is no God" [Psalm 14:1]. "After your own eyes:" this refers to the hankering after immorality; and so it says, "And Samson said to his father, 'Get her for me, for she is pleasing in my eyes'" [Judges 14:3]. "After which ye use to go astray:" this refers to the hankering after idolatry; and so it says, "And they went astray after the Baalim" [Judges 8:33]. (b.*Berachot* 12b)

Instead the Torah calls us to follow God's instructions no matter what the circumstances or how we might feel about it. Right and wrong are not based on one's opinions or feelings but on HaShem's desires as they are laid out in his Torah. Rabbi Hirsch continues:

> Then we feel at one with God, and we no longer feel that power or greatness lie in satisfying our senses or the dictates of our minds, but in the exertion of our moral will, which will we will have absorbed into the will of God.[75]

This is the same idea that the Master talks about with dying to ourselves and taking up our cross daily (Matthew 16:24–25). When we set aside our will for his, he draws us ever closer into his presence. For the Jewish people, the tzitzit provide a continuous reminder of the commandments as well as a reminder not to let one's own emotions and desires dictate one's life.

A ROYAL PRIESTHOOD

> So you shall remember and do all my commandments, and be holy to your God. (Numbers 15:40)

There are some clues within the commandment of the tzitzit that it is meant to be a sort of priestly garment. First there is the injunction of the thread of *techelet*. As we noted this is a specific shade of blue that was quite costly and usually could only be afforded by the rich. This same shade of blue also appears in the garments of the priests:

> And they shall make the ephod of gold, of blue (*techelet*) and purple and scarlet yarns, and of fine twined linen, skillfully worked. (Exodus 28:6)

> And the sash of fine twined linen and of blue (*techelet*) and purple and scarlet yarns, embroidered with needlework, as the LORD had commanded Moses. (Exodus 39:29)

In fact the very phrase "cord of blue" (*petil techelet*, פתיל תכלת) appears in connection with the high priest's turban: "And you shall fasten [the gold plate] on the turban by a cord of blue" (Exodus 28:37). *Techelet* also appears in the tapestry of the tabernacle.[76]

Techelet was also a sign of royalty and nobility:

> Then Mordecai went out from the presence of the king in royal robes of blue (*techelet*) and white. (Esther 8:15)

In addition to the *techelet* another indication of the priest-like status of the tzitzit is the traditional presence of *sha'atnez* (שעטנז). As we pointed out above, *sha'atnez* is the mixture of wool and linen that is strictly prohibited by the Torah for the garments of the average Israelite.[77] Yet, the mixture of wool and linen was commanded to be present in the tapestries of the tabernacle and the garments of the priests.[78] We know this because the fabrics were to be made from colored materials as well as linen; for example the Tabernacle coverings (Exodus 26:1) and the High Priest's ephod (Exodus 28:6). Linen was very difficult to dye and therefore almost all colored materials were made of wool.[79]

Surprisingly in rabbinic literature the rabbis see the Torah as allowing *sha'atnez* to be present in tzitzit.[80] It is highly unlikely that the rabbis would create an injunction which so blatantly contradicted a biblical commandment, so what was their reasoning? Firstly the commandants of tzitzit and *sha'atnez* appear back to back in Deuteronomy 22:11–12.[81] The sages wondered why the Torah repeated the prohibition of *sha'atnez* once again. What new thing do we learn? Rashi also points out the strange order of the noun *gedilim* ("tassel") before the verb.[82] The final conclusion of the sages is brought out in an ancient *Targum Yonatan*:

You shall not clothe nor warm yourselves with a garment combed (carded) or netted, or interwoven with woolen and linen mixed together. Nevertheless on a robe of linen thread you may be permitted to make fringes of woolen upon the four extremities of your vestments with which you dress in the day. (*Targum Yonatan* to Deuteronomy 22:12)

This verse was therefore interpreted by the sages as permitting the mixture of wool and linen on tzitzit if necessary. Since linen could not be dyed, a four-cornered linen garment necessarily required at least a single thread of wool in order to fulfill the *techelet*-blue requirement. The garment of the poor man was usually made of linen.

The tassel with a thread of blue signified more than royalty or nobility, however. It also signified the priesthood. We may assume that the thread of blue was made of wool. The ancients had great difficulty in dying linen because the colors would run, so all dyed garments are assumed to be wool. A poor man's garment was commonly made of flax, that is, linen—not the fine, expensive linen worn by the priests (called *ses* or *bus*) but the coarse, inexpensive type spun on home looms. In Canaan after the Israelite settlement, the people subsisted on a predominantly agricultural economy, and where agriculture predominated, flax was the common cloth. Rehab's hiding of the spies at Jericho under stalks of flax (Joshua 2:6) is evidence that flax was indigenous to Canaan.[83]

Further evidence for this practice is found in the excavations of the Bar Kochba caves. Archaeologists found threads, intended for tying tzitzit. The threads consisted of white linen and wool *techelet*.[84]

Why then would God allow a forbidden mixture of wool and linen in the tzitzit? Because it is not as much forbidden as it is a sign of holiness. Deuteronomy 22:9 states: "You shall not sow your vineyard with two kinds of seed, lest the whole yield be forfeited." The word for fortified in Hebrew is *kadash* (קדש) which means "holy, set apart." Here in this verse it has the sense of "dedicated to the sanctuary."[85] The Tabernacle and the priests were set apart for service–the service of HaShem. In turn, when the Torah allows Israel to mix wool and linen in the tzitzit, it imparts to them a little bit of the holiness of the Tabernacle and priesthood. "Thus we learn that fringes add holiness to Israel" (*Sifre* 115).[86]

The *techelet* in the garment of the layman reminds him that Israel is to be "a kingdom of priests and a holy nation" (Exodus 19:6). In a previous chapter we discussed the cultural background of the tzitzit in the ancient Near East and how an elaborate hem was a sign of prestige. Thus, *techelet* in the tzitzit of the average Israelite indicates that HaShem thinks very highly of his people.

In fact we find that exact language at the end of commandment of tzitzit where the Torah states: "So you shall remember and do all my commandments, and be holy to your God" (Numbers 15:40). HaShem desires that Israel be set apart unto him. The tzitzit are a reminder of the status and calling Israel has in God's eyes. Even non-Jewish believers are called to the spiritual priesthood in Messiah. The Master's chief disciple writes to Gentile believers:

> You yourselves like living stones are being built up as a spiritual house, to be a holy priesthood, to offer spiritual sacrifices acceptable to God through Messiah Yeshua. … But you are a chosen race, a royal priesthood, a holy nation, a people for his own possession, that you may proclaim the excellencies of him who called you out of darkness into his marvelous light. (1 Peter 2:5–9)

Salvation

> I am the LORD your God, who brought you out of the land of Egypt to be your God: I am the LORD your God." (Numbers 15:41)

At the end of the passage about the tzitzit, the Torah reminds us that HaShem brought the Jewish people out of Egypt and that he is Israel's God. The Exodus from Egypt established an eternal bond between HaShem and his people. Rabbi Aryeh Kaplan writes: "The unique miracles of the Exodus had the specific purpose—to forge this bond between God and Israel. God therefore repeats, 'I am God your Lord'—now and forever."[87]

HaShem revealed his Torah to Israel on the strength of that bond, but only after the salvation from Egypt. The Torah includes the commandment of tzitzit which represents all of the other 612 commandments because the tzitzit are a reminder of all of them. Thus the tzitzit uniquely represent the new life and relationship the Jewish people have with the Creator:

> Once the Torah was given at Sinai, actual performance of the positive mitzvos, and refraining from transgressing the prohibitions, must always be our primary consideration.[88]

Israel's deliverance from Egypt finds an additional meaning as a foreshadowing of the salvation now found in our Master Yeshua. Thus, just as the tzitzit are a reminder of Israel's exodus from Egypt, they are also a reminder of the new life and freedom from sin that the disciple gains through Messiah's atoning death. And just as it was for Israel after leaving Egypt, the new life in Messiah requires making choices and walking in obedience—tasks which the tzitzit can help guide.

A Part of God

> Then the LORD God formed man of dust from the ground, and breathed into his nostrils the breath of life [*neshamah*, נשמה]; and man became a living creature. (Genesis 2:7)

Judaism teaches that the godly soul leaves its abode in the heavens to inhabit an earthly body. This descent of the soul is derived from a mystical reading of Genesis 2:7 where HaShem breathes life into Adam.

The Hebrew word for "breath" is *neshamah* (נשמה). The same word is commonly used in Judaism to refer to the divine soul. By reading *neshamah* as soul, one may understand the "breath of life" that God breathed into Adam as the divine, pre-existent soul being imparted into human flesh and binding to the body.[89] Thus in a sense everyone has a piece of the divine inside of them.

Chassidic Judaism sees the *tzitzit* as symbolic of this inner, divine spark:

> The essence-character of the Jewish person is beyond estimation and assessment, for he is a part of (G-d's) Essence, and whoever lays hold of a part of The Essence is as though he lays hold of it all. Just as The Essence is unlimited, so is the part unlimited. This is similar to *tzitzit* being "on the corner"—i.e., "of the same material as the corner" of the garment. (The existence of the soul as an entity discrete from G-d's Essence) is only because G-d created the soul to be a *created* being. (*HaYom Yom*, Kislev 13)[90]

Just as the tzitzit is of the same material as the garment itself to which it is attached but yet distinct, so too every human being contains the essence of God yet is distinct from him.

Garments of Light

> Bless the LORD, O my soul! O LORD my God, you are very great! You are clothed with splendor and majesty, covering yourself with light as with a garment, stretching out the heavens like a tent. (Psalm 104:1–2)

This verse is interpreted by the sages of Israel as referring to the creation of the world.

> And God said: Let there be light, etc. Rabbi Simeon ben Rabbi Jehozadak asked Rabbi Samuel ben Nahman: "As I have heard that you are a master of haggadah, tell me when the light was created?" He replied: "The Holy One, blessed be he, wrapped himself therein as in a tallit and irradiated with the luster of his majesty the whole world from one end to the other." … whereupon he observed, "There is a verse which states it explicitly: Who covers yourself with light as with a garment (Psalm 104:2). (*Genesis Rabbah* 3:4)

The *Midrash* paints a picture of HaShem wrapping himself in tallit as he shines forth the brilliance of his light at the very creation of the universe.

As the mystics of Israel mused over the meaning of the tzitzit and the tallit, they began to see them as not just reminders of this world but of the World to Come.

They saw the tallit and tzitzit as esoteric garments which prepared man for the entrance into the World to Come.

To the mystics, the tallit with the tzitzit symbolized the garments of righteousness in the World to Come, and they represented the splendid garments of HaShem's light. Rebbe Nachman stated that the tzitzit "represent the light of truth,"[91] and Rebbe Menachem Mendel taught that the tallit is "[the garment] spread out by the King" which alludes to the revelation of this encompassing light," i.e., the light of Godly revelation.[92] Chassidic Judaism teaches that these symbols come alive as one prepares for the morning prayers and wraps himself in his tallit.

> When you put on your tallit you should think that the light of the Infinite One is hidden within this tallit that you wrap yourself in… and when the wings of the tallit cover you, you are covered in the wings of the Infinite One. (*Or haGanuz l'Tzaddikim*, 36)[93]

The tallit represents HaShem's covering over the petitioner and becomes a visible picture of coming into the presence of God and being enveloped by his light. It gives a visible and tangible picture of the Psalmist's words "in the shadow of your wings I will take refuge" (Psalm 57:1). As the petitioner wraps himself in his tallit it gives him a sense of the protective covering of the Father.

Even the two separate aspects of the tallit (i.e., the tallit itself and the tzitzit) represent how HaShem comes to meet with us. The tallit represents the fullness of God which is lofty and unknowable, but the tzitzit themselves dangle down to us, representing the small part of God that we can know. The tzitzit represent how HaShem does indeed desire to reach into our words and be a part of us.

It then takes only a short leap to imagine that this also represents the Father's covering in the sense of protection as well.

The meaning of the *tallit* is that of something which covers and surrounds—the secret of a great surrounding light—for the surrounding light [of God] protects a person from every evil … and he is saved from the wayward influence of [negative forces]. (*Kitzur Shnei Luchot haBrit, Mesechet Holin, Inyanin Tzitzit*, 18)[94]

God's presence is always with his children protecting them from danger and disaster, and the tallit is a picture of that covering. Some of the sages even compared the tefillin and the tzitzit to "weapons to pay suit to the Holy King" that prepare one for the battles of the day.[95] This is reminiscent of the Apostle Paul's words about putting "on the whole armor of God, that you may be able to stand against the schemes of the devil" (Ephesians 6:11).

TAKE HOLD

Before we leave the subject of the symbolism of tzitzit, consider one last prophetic picture. In Zechariah 8:23 we read:

> Thus says the LORD of hosts: In those days ten men from the nations of every tongue shall take hold of the robe of a Jew, saying, "Let us go with you, for we have heard that God is with you."

The prophet is looking toward the messianic future. He foresees the coming day when King Messiah is ruling out of Jerusalem and all nations will make pilgrimage to Zion to seek the LORD. In the prophecy, ten men from all nations take hold of the garment of a single Jew. As we have pointed out, the word for "robe" in Zechariah 8:23 is *kanaf*, which is the corner of the garment where the tzitzit are attached.

In Judaism, ten is the minimum number of men necessary to constitute a congregation. Ten men form a *minyan* (מנין). So we might read this prophecy as saying, "A congregation from all nations." Rabbi David Kimchi comments on this verse:

> "Ten men."—Ten is not to be taken strictly, but it is a round number, like *"Ten women shall bake your bread,"* and other similar passages. And according to the Drash: "Ten men

out of all the languages of the nations" means 700 to each skirt of the Arbah Kanphoth (four corners) [for a total of 2,800].[96]

Thus Zechariah 8:23 is an apt description for the greater Body of Messiah, which is made up of a congregation from all nations. The single Jew can be understood to be Messiah. He is the quintessential Jew who represents the whole of Israel—the singular "seed" of the patriarchs. He is *the* Jew. The picture then would be that of the Gentiles (nations) laying hold of Messiah. Thus the tzitzit also represent all of the non-Jews throughout history who have taken hold of Messiah and have become grafted into the commonwealth of Israel.

6
The Nature of Tzitzit

As we have mentioned already the actual practice of the tzitzit takes on two separate forms. The *tallit katan* is worn under one's clothes all day long with the tzitzit either pulled out or tucked in depending upon one's custom,[97] and the *tallit gadol* which is worn by Jewish men during morning prayers both on weekdays and Shabbat. In both cases the tzitzit are identical, so let's begin by discussing the makeup of the actual tzitzit.

TZITZIT

> The LORD said to Moses, "Speak to the people of Israel, and tell them to make tassels on the corners of their garments throughout their generations, and to put a cord of blue on the tassel of each corner. (Numbers 15:37–38)

A cursory reading of this passage suggests that the tzitzit was some sort of tassel which contained a thread of blue. Simple. Thus some are quick to dismiss the rabbinic rulings as mere "traditions of men." Yet, upon a closer examination of the text we can see that many of the enactments of the sages surrounding the tzitzit are rooted firmly within the Torah.

As we mentioned earlier, the passage in Numbers uses the word *tzitzit* which means "tassel," but the passage in Deuteronomy uses the word *gedilim* which means "twists" or "braids of thread." The two words are reconciled in the actual traditional practice. Tradition requires a top knotted section of the tassel, which satisfies the definition of *gedilim*, and it requires the bottom half of the tassel to be loose strings, which satisfies the definition of *tzitzit*.[98] The section of loose string on the bottom is referred to as the *anaf* (אנף).

So how should the braided section be created? The Torah tells us "to put a *petil techelet* on the tassel of each corner." The word *petil* (פתיל) is translated in the ESV as "cord." *Petil* can also be translated as "twist," which Aryeh Kaplan points out has several implications.[99] Foremost, it indicates that one string should be wound around the rest, and that is why the Torah states that the "cord of blue" should be "on the tassel." In other words, the blue thread should be wrapped around the hanging threads to create a *gedilim* (braided) section. Today, most Jews no longer use a blue thread. A white thread is used in its place. When a blue thread is used, it should be the one that is wrapped around the others.

The word *petil* also teaches us that the actual strings themselves should be made out of two strings that are twisted together. Because *petil* can also connote "joined" or "bent," it teaches that the strings used in the tzitzit must be doubled over.[100]

When the sages defined the word *gedilim* even further, they found the requirement that the tzitzit must contain four threads. Rabbi Kaplan writes:

> The *Gedil* means hairs or strings bound together to form a tassel, braid or rope. Obviously a single string, even if doubled and twisted, would not be called *Gedil* or tassel. (As we have already seen, the word *Petil* already has this connotation.) It must therefore refer to a minimum of two doubled strings. The word used in the Torah—*Gedilim*—is plural; therefore must be a "doubled tassel" on each corner. This is an allusion to the fact that the Tzitzith must contain

four doubled strings. *Gedil* in singular is two, and *Gedilim* in plural is four.[101]

Hence the sages find the injunction to have four strings in each tzitzit. Each string is then doubled over to make eight ends. Then one string is wrapped around the others in various ways with accompanying knots, depending upon the tradition being followed. In the end, the sages decided that the knotted/braided section should constitute one-third of the entire tzitzit.[102]

Most of the ancient traditions, with the notable exception of the Yemenites, specify five knots in the upper section of the tzitzit. This tradition is ancient. It even appears in *Targum Pseudo Yonatan* to Numbers 15:38. Different teachers offer various explanations of the symbolism. The five knots might represent the five books of the Torah, or they might be a reminder that all five senses should be dedicated unto HaShem, and so forth.[103]

The number of windings between the knots is not specified by the Torah. Thus the sages only require one *chulya* (חוליא), i.e., the "section of the fringe around which a thread has been wound several times, and bounded at each end by a knot."[104] Today, the number of windings and loops depends upon which tradition one is following.

The only color requirement of the tzitzit is for the "cord of blue (*petil techelet*)." Nevertheless, the other strings should be white. Today most of practicing Judaism wears all white tzitzit. Even for those who do wear the *techelet* thread, the rest of their tzitzit are white. The Rambam raises the point that the tzitzit is called white "because we are not commanded to dye it."[105] Some halachic authorities feel that the tzitzit should only be white based on the verse in Daniel 7:9, "his clothing was white as snow," which is interpreted as referring to HaShem's tallit.[106]

The Rambam brings up another tradition of dyeing the tzitzit to match whatever color the garment itself was.[107] An opinion in the Talmud even mandates that the non-*techelet* threads of the tzitzit should be the same color as the garment.[108] The reason for this ruling can be found in Numbers 15:39 where the Torah refers to the combination of the garment and the tzitzit as "it," (*oto*, אתו). Jacob Milgrom points out: "Hebrew *'oto*, masculine, cannot refer to the tassel, which is a feminine noun, but must refer to the entire combination of tassel and thread."[109] Because the Torah referred to the garment and the tzitzit as one single unit, some ruled that they should be the same color.[110]

Today, the majority of observant Jews try to fulfill both rulings by having the *tallit gadol* or *tallit katan* white as well as all non-*techelet* strings white as well.[111] The tzitzit strings themselves can be made from wool or flax.[112] The halachic requirement for the length of the *tziztzit* today is set at twelve *agudalot* ("fingerbreadths," אגו־דלות) which is approximately between nine and ten inches.[113]

Techelet

> The LORD said to Moses, "Speak to the people of Israel, and tell them to … put a cord of blue (*petil techelet*, תכלת פתיל) on the tassel of each corner." (Numbers 15:37–38)

The Torah commands that each of the tzitzit contain a cord of a blue called *techelet*. The Rambam viewed the requirement of the cord of *techelet* and the tzitzit as two separate injunctions that encompassed one *mitzvah*.

Techelet is not a general word for the color blue; it refers to a specific dye. *Techelet* was used to dye wool. It was the dye of the rich as it was extremely expensive. The Talmud attests to its expensive nature and relates a legend that the rare and precious dye comes only from a marine animal called the *chillazon* (חילזון) which only appears once every seventy years.[114] Indeed, the dye of *techelet* has had quite a history among the Jewish people.

The priceless nature of the *techelet* led some merchants in the Talmudic age to pass off a dye from the *Kela Ilan* ("True Indigo," קלא אילן) plant as *techelet* and thus trick Jews into believing they were purchasing the real thing.[115] The sages prohibited using the *Kela Ilan* or anything other than true *techelet*. They ruled that if one did not have *techelet* they should simply use white.[116]

The poverty of the Jewish people at the time and the possibility of purchasing artificial *techelet* led the rabbis to suspend the requirement of *techelet* in tzitzit. Jacob Milgrom gives more background:

The requirement of the violet cord was suspended in rabbinic times. The Jewish community following the two
Roman wars was so impoverished that many could not
afford even the one violet-dyed cord required for each
tsitsit. Moreover, the dye industry apparently declined and
the *tekhelet* became scarce. To be sure, a cheap counterfeit
had been developed from the indigo plant but the rabbis
disqualified it as a *tekhelet*. These factors contributed to
the suspension of the violet cord requirement, and since
then *tsitsit* have been totally white.[117]

The counterfeits were becoming more and more popular for
two reasons. First, the Jewish people simply could not afford even a
small amount of the authentic *techelet*. As Milgrom pointed out, the
two unsuccessful revolts against Rome had left the Jewish communities in a dire state of poverty. Second, the price of this dye went up
and up as production declined. Eventually, the precise identification of the *chillazon*—the source of the dye—was forgotten as well.

Some might feel that this means that the rabbis' ruling over-
rode the commandment to have a thread of blue in the tzitzit and is
therefore abolishing the Torah. Rather, the sages upheld the Torah
by prohibiting the use of counterfeit *techelet*. They knew that people
would be inclined to use substitutions, but substitutions do not
fulfill the commandment and they cheapen the meaning of true
techelet. Other people might attempt to purchase the true *techelet*
at extreme expense and hardship, or worse yet, be tempted to purchase the imitation *techelet,* thus violating the Torah. Therefore,
they ruled to protect both the authenticity of the commandment
and human dignity; they felt it was better to do half of the *mitzvah*
correctly rather than to do all of it incorrectly.

Yet, almost two thousand years later, there has been a major
attempt within Orthodox Judaism to rediscover the true source of
the *techelet*. Within the last two hundred years, the Jewish world
has made an effort to once again correctly identify the *chillazon*.
Rabbis and scientists worked together combining an intense study
of rabbinic texts with a scientific examination of the ancient dying
process. Not surprisingly, a few different opinions have emerged.

While all opinions agree that the *chillazon* is a type of mollusk, there are three different opinions as to what species it is precisely. The three prevailing opinions are the *Sepia officinalis*, which is commonly known as the Cuttlefish; *Janthina*, commonly known as the Purple Snail; and the *Murex trunculus* (*Hexaplex trunculus*), also known as the Banded Dye-Murex. Of the three, the *Murex trunculus* looks to be the correct candidate. In 2011, scientists chemically analyzed a piece of the *techelet* found in the Bar Kochba caves and determined that the source of the dye was the *Murex trunculus*.[118]

Although most observant Jews still do not wear *techelet* today due to the remaining uncertainty over the identification of the *chilazon*, it is gaining more and more popularity. Many chasidic Jews of the Breslov persuasion have adopted it, particularly those who live in Israel. It is exciting to see a renaissance of such an important mitzvah. Something that had been lost for almost two millennia has returned. HaShem is restoring those things which have been lost and forgotten.

Practically, when the *techelet* is worn, the majority opinion holds that only one of the four strings that make up the *tzitzit* should be dyed blue.[119] This ruling is based on the word *petil* ("cord") which appears as a singular noun in Numbers 15:38.The antiquity of the one-string-dyed tradition is verified by the tzitzit from the Bar Kochba excavations where only one of the strings is dyed with *techelet*.[120] Rabbinic authorities also differ as to whether or not the entire string should be dyed blue or just half.[121]

TALLIT KATAN

> You shall make yourself tassels on the four corners of the garment with which you cover yourself. (Deuteronomy 22:12)

According to the Torah, only a four-cornered garment actually requires tzitzit.[122] The Torah explicitly says "on the four corners (*arba kanfot*, ארבע כנפות) of the garment." On this basis, tzitzit are not worn on garments without four corners. After people no longer wore four-cornered garments, the tzitzit were relegated to ritual garments: the prayer shawl and the *tallit katan*.

The *tallit katan* ("small tallit") was created to be worn under one's clothes so that the commandment of tzitzit could still be carried out during the day. The *tallit katan* (also called an *arba kanfot*) can be made of wool, linen, or cotton and, according to halachah, should be at least an *amah* (cubit) squared, that is 18 to 24 inches.[123] It then has a rectangular or circular hole cut in the top where the head comes through. The tzitzit are attached to holes at the four corners.

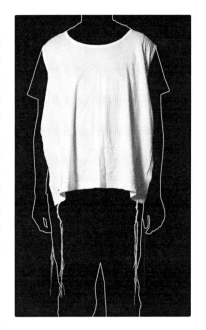

TALLIT GADOL

While the smaller *tallit katan* is worn under one's clothes all day, the *tallit gadol* ("large tallit") is worn primarily during morning prayers. It can be thought of as the last surviving relic of the original tallit from the biblical and rabbinic periods.

Unlike the *tallit katan*, most *tallitot* today are made of pure white wool and many contain black or blue stripes that are said to be reminders of the *techelet*. In general they should be large enough to drape over one's shoulder with two sets of tzitzit in front and two in back.[124] Some *tallitot* have an ornate crown (*atarah*, עֲטָרָה) across the top marking which part is placed over the head.

7
Non-Jews and Tzitzit

The commandment of tzitzit was specifically given to "sons of Israel," that is Jewish men (Numbers 15:38). It is one of the sign (*ot*, אות) commandments that have distinguished the Jewish people from the nations for thousands of years. The tzitzit are the unequivocal sign of an observant Jewish male. The mitzvah's ongoing validity for Jewish believers in Messiah is demonstrated not only in Messiah's incredibly strong words about the Torah not being abolished but in the example he sets by wearing tzitzit himself. So where does this leave Gentile believers? Although they have not been explicitly commanded to wear tzitzit, is it permissible for them to participate in the mitzvah?

JEWISH SOURCES

We will begin answering this question by examining what Jewish sources say about the topic. The earliest reference to Gentiles and tzitzit is found in a passage of the Talmud.

> Our Rabbis taught: If a man bought a garment furnished with tzitzit from an Israelite in the market, the presumption is [that it is valid]; if he bought it from a gentile, who was a merchant, it is valid, but if he was a private individual it is invalid. And [this is so] not withstanding that they said, A man may not sell a garment furnished with tzitzit to a gentile unless he removed the tzitzit. What is the reason for this?—Here it was explained, on account of a harlot. Rab Judah said, It is to be feared that [an Israelite] might join him on the road and he might kill him. (b.*Menachot* 43a)[125]

The first part of the passage deals with Jews purchasing tzitzit from Gentiles. According to the passage, it is permissible for a Jew to buy tzitzit from a Gentile if it is in a marketplace because it is assumed that he will not risk his reputation as a merchant and sell halachically invalid tzitzit. Whereas if it is an individual who is not a store owner, he cannot be trusted. The background of this prohibition was the frequent deception of Jews by Gentiles in the marketplace during the rabbinic era. There was money to be made in counterfeit *techelet*.

The second section deals with selling a Gentile tzitzit. This is forbidden based on two reasons: The first is that the Gentile might try to either pay off a harlot with the garment thus making it look as though it was a Jewish man who committed the sin. The second is that the Gentile might disguise himself as a Jew in order to deceive other Jews. The Talmudic example of a Gentile who disguises himself for the purpose of murdering a Jew is extreme, but in reality the deception could be for any number of reasons.

What is most significant for us is what the passage does not say. It is does not say that Jews should not sell tzitzit to non-Jews because it is forbidden for Gentiles to wear them. In fact rabbinic literature does not contain a specific ruling that Gentiles should not wear tzitzit.

This passage also shows that Gentiles wanted to purchase tzitzit and that this was widespread enough that a halachic ruling needed to be made. Although they could have wanted to purchase them for deception as the Talmud indicates or simply to sell them again, this might even indicate that some non-Jews who were close to Jewish communities were wearing them.

Generations later in the writings of the Rambam we find this intriguing passage:

> Women and servants who wish to wrap themselves in tzitzit may do so without reciting a blessing. (*Hilchot Tzitzit* 3:9)[126]

The "servants" referred to are Gentile servants. They, like woman, would not be obligated to observe the commandment of tzitzit.[127] Thus if these non-Jewish servants choose to observe the commandment of tzitzit, they are permitted to do so but without reciting the blessing, which says, "who has commanded us concerning tzitzit."

Elsewhere in the *Mishneh Torah* the Rambam states:

> We should not prevent a gentile who desires to perform one of the Torah's mitzvot in order to receive reward from doing so, [provided] he performs it as required. (*Hilchot Melachim* 10:10)[128]

The Rambam sees that when Gentiles take on additional mitzvot that are not commanded to them, they can receive a blessing.[129] In a similar fashion Rabbi Chaim Kanievsky, a world-renowned modern-day Israeli Haredi *posek* ("legal authority") ruled that a Gentile who has taken upon himself the "seven laws of Noah" may then take upon himself any other *mitzvah* of Torah.[130] When we couple this passage from the *Mishneh Torah* with the one about slaves wearing tzitzit, it seems reasonable to assume that the Rambam would have permitted non-Jews to wear tzitzit, albeit without reciting the blessing.[131]

While it is technically not forbidden, many in modern-day Judaism frown upon Gentiles wearing tzitzit.[132] Rav Moshe Feinstein writes:

> But regarding Sabbath and Yom Tov observance and laying tefillin, and wearing *tzitzit* … and all similar manners, a non-Jew would receive no reward for such observance, because non-Jews are excluded from these mitzvot, since they did not receive the Torah, and these are not considered mitzvot for them.[133]

As we said, wearing tzitzit is considered to be a demarcation between Jews and Gentiles. Many feel that non-Jews wearing tzitzit blur this line. Although Gentiles are not forbidden from wearing them, most modern-day rabbis would discourage it. Non-Jews need to be sensitive to Jewish sentiment and propriety as they consider the idea of wearing tzitzit.

The Apostles

Turning now to the Apostolic Writings, we see that neither Yeshua nor the apostles ever directly applied the mitzvah of tzitzit to Gentiles. Certainly the discussions and rulings of Acts 15 exempt Gentiles from the mitzvah of tzitzit, as it is one of the sign commandments distinct to the Jewish people and not included in the four essentials of the Jerusalem Council.

On the one hand Gentile believers have become part of the larger spiritual commonwealth of Israel.[134] This status may put them into a different category than the Gentile outside of Messiah to which the rabbis mentioned above are directing their halachic rulings. Needless to say, the rabbinic world does not acknowledge Gentile faith in Yeshua as a factor in their decisions.

On the other hand there is still a distinction. Paul tells us that in Messiah there is "neither Jew nor Greek, there is neither slave nor free, there is no male nor female" (Galatians 3:28). Yet this verse does not eliminate the physical differences between Jew and Gentile any more than it does between male and female. While we are all one in Messiah, we all have our separate roles. The Jewish people have a unique calling before God to be Jews, while believers from the nations have their own paths to walk. Therefore when discussing Gentiles wearing tzitzit we also need to bear this reality in mind.

Some Practical Advice

As a non-Jewish follower of the Master myself, I have chosen to implement the practice of tzitzit in my life. Although the tzitzit for me as a non-Jew are not obligatory, I find the discipline rewarding. Its symbolism gives me a sense of solidarity with Israel and the Jewish community. At the same time I realize that, for Gentiles, the practice of tzitzit can be fraught with pitfalls. Let me illustrate with a story.

I grew up on the East Coast as an avid New York Mets baseball fan. That meant I had two favorite teams, the Mets and whoever was playing the Yankees. One summer while attending a baseball game in Colorado there was a man at the game with a Mets hat and a Yankees jersey. He got quite a few funny looks and I overheard a number of people make comments under their breath such as "He's a poser." We all knew nothing about this man except one thing; he was obviously not from New York.

Such can often be the case for the Hebrew-roots Gentile who goes out into public wearing the signs of Jewish identity. Too many times, well-meaning Gentile believers in Messiah take a mitzvah such as tzitzit and run with it. Whether it's adding crazy colors to the tzitzit, attaching them to one's belt loops or key chains, wearing them without a head covering, or even using them to convince themselves and others that they are Jewish, it comes across as disingenuous and, frankly speaking, silly looking. I think the Jewish community begins to view us much like how the fans viewed the mixed-up Mets-Yankees fan. In an effort to be a part of the "in-crowd" and do the right thing, the Gentile Christian's zeal for his Hebrew roots has created just the opposite effect.

I'd like to offer a few guidelines to help prevent these sorts of pitfalls. First and foremost, if a Gentile decides to take on the practice of tzitzit, it should be done in the traditional manner, with sensitivity to the rulings of the rabbis. Judaism has preserved rich and beautiful traditions in the *tallit gadol* and the *tallit katan*. Gentile believers like myself would be foolish to try and reinvent the wheel. Rather, it would behoove us to honor the family that we have become a part of.

Second, a Gentile believer who wears a *tallit katan* throughout the day would be well served to tuck in his tzitzit so they are out of sight and not attracting attention. It also might be best to reserve the use of a *tallit gadol* for the privacy of his personal prayer time. As we have stated, tzitzit are a visible sign to both the world and other Jews that one is Jewish (and for that matter practicing Orthodox Judaism). Wearing them visibly can be like false advertising, and it communicates disrespect for the Jewish people. The Jewish community generally perceives Gentiles wearing tzitzit or praying with a *tallit gadol* in public as offensive. It looks like deception to Jews, and to non-Jewish believers, it looks something like kids playing cowboy—dressing up Jewish. Additionally when Gentiles wear visible tzitzit and do things that violate Orthodox tradition it can be a stumbling block rather than an opportunity to witness to the Jewish people as some might think. While I do not want to be dogmatic, non-Jews who take up this mitzvah should consider keeping its observance private, tucking their tzitzit in, and refraining from wearing a *tallit gadol* during public services.

Third, as we have pointed out, the tzitzit are a reminder to obey the commandants of the Torah. Therefore, it would behoove a non-Jewish believer to actually know the commandments that apply to him as a Gentile along with all their implications before wearing something that is supposed to remind him of that. So often, tzitzit becomes the first mitzvah that believers studying their Hebrew roots decide to take on. It can quickly become a way to show off what one is learning to other believers. Just as our Master instructed in Matthew 23:5 we must never turn the fulfillment of mitzvot into pretentiousness.

For Gentile believers, when the mitzvah of tzitzit is observed in a manner sensitive to greater Judaism and in a manner that preserves distinction, it can be a beautiful reminder of who they are in Messiah and of his call to righteous living. Non-Jews are free to embrace this mitzvah, but they are not less in the eyes of God if they choose not to do so. If you are a Gentile considering the mitzvah of tzitzit, it might be best to seek the council of one's local Messianic Jewish rabbi before deciding whether or not to apply this mitzvah.

8
Conclusion

Although we have touched on many aspects of the tzitzit throughout this book, we have for the most part avoided providing specific halachah guidelines. For those interested in these details and to learn more about tzitzit in general I recommend the following resources:

- Kaplan, Rabbi Aryeh. *Tzitzith: A Thread of Light*. New York: National Conference of Synagogue Youth, 1991.

- Maimonides, Moses. *Maimonides Mishneh Torah: Hilchot Tefillin UMezuzah V'Sefer Torah Hilchot Tzitzit*. Translated by Rabbi Eliyahu Touger; Jerusalem: Moznaim Publishing, 1988.

- Cohen, Rabbi Simcha Bunim. *Laws of Daily Living: Volume One*. Brooklyn, NY: Mesorah Publications, 2007.

I hope that this small book has served as a useful introduction to the mitzvah of tzitzit. Far from being a simple outward command, its function and symbolism touch on some of the deepest spiritual truths of the Scriptures. I pray that this study will serve as an opportunity for further exploration and strengthen your relationship with our Father in heaven and his Son Yeshua.

May we all bask in the splendor and majesty of HaShem's light as he spreads out his tallit in the heavens like a tent (Psalm 104:1–2). Amen!

Tzitzit Blessings

PUTTING ON THE TZITZIT

Recite this blessing when putting on the small four-cornered undergarment known as a *tallit katan*. One who wears a *tallit gadol*, a full prayer shawl, should skip this blessing and recite the blessing for wearing a *tallit* at the time that he puts it on.

בָּרוּךְ אַתָּה יְיָ אֱלֹהֵינוּ
מֶלֶךְ הָעוֹלָם, אֲשֶׁר קִדְּשָׁנוּ
בְּמִצְוֹתָיו, וְצִוָּנוּ עַל מִצְוַת
צִיצִת.

Baruch attah ADONAI eloheinu
melech ha'olam, asher kiddeshanu
bemitzvotav, vetzivanu al mitzvat
tzitzit.

Blessed are you, O LORD, our God, King of the universe, who has sanctified us with his commandments and has commanded us about the commandment of *tzitzit*.

PUTTING ON THE TALLIT

One should stand when putting on a *tallit*. As you recite this paragraph, examine each *tzitzit* on the *tallit* to make sure that they are intact and not tangled or torn.

בָּרְכִי נַפְשִׁי אֶת יְיָ, יְיָ
אֱלֹהַי גָּדַלְתָּ מְּאֹד, הוֹד וְהָדָר
לָבֵשְׁתָּ. עֹטֶה אוֹר כַּשַּׂלְמָה,
נוֹטֶה שָׁמַיִם כַּיְרִיעָה.

Barechi nafshi et ADONAI, ADONAI elohai
gadalta me'od, hod vehadar lavasheta.
Oteh or kasalmah,
noteh shamayim kayri'ah.

Bless the LORD, my soul! O LORD, my God, you are very great. You are clothed with beauty and splendor, wrapped in light like a robe, spreading out heaven like a curtain.

Hold the tallit up in preparation to wrap yourself with it.

בָּרוּךְ אַתָּה יְיָ אֱלֹהֵינוּ
מֶלֶךְ הָעוֹלָם, אֲשֶׁר קִדְּשָׁנוּ
בְּמִצְוֹתָיו, וְצִוָּנוּ לְהִתְעַטֵּף
בַּצִּיצִת.

Baruch attah ADONAI eloheinu
melech ha'olam, asher kiddeshanu
bemitzvotav, vetzivanu lehit'attef
batzitzit.

Blessed are you, O LORD, our God, King of the universe, who has sanctified us with his commandments, and has commanded us to wrap ourselves in *tzitzit*.

Wrap your head and body with the tallit. Some have the custom of gathering the four corners of the tallit and placing them over the left shoulder while reciting the final passage.

מַה יָּקָר חַסְדְּךָ אֱלֹהִים, וּבְנֵי
אָדָם בְּצֵל כְּנָפֶיךָ יֶחֱסָיוּן.
יִרְוְיֻן מִדֶּשֶׁן בֵּיתֶךָ,
וְנַחַל עֲדָנֶיךָ תַשְׁקֵם.
כִּי עִמְּךָ מְקוֹר חַיִּים,
בְּאוֹרְךָ נִרְאֶה אוֹר. מְשֹׁךְ
חַסְדְּךָ לְיֹדְעֶיךָ,
וְצִדְקָתְךָ לְיִשְׁרֵי לֵב.

Mah yakar chasdecha elohim, uvenei
adam betzel kenafeicha yechesayun.
Yirveyun mideshen beitecha,
venachal adaneicha tashkem.
Ki immecha mekor chayim,
be'orecha nir'eh or. Meshoch
chasdecha leyode'eicha,
vetzidkatecha leyishrei lev.

How precious is your devotion, O God! Human beings take refuge in the shadow of your wings. They drink deeply from the richness of your house, and you let them drink from the river of your delights. The fountain of life is with you; in your light, we will see light. Extend your devotion to those who know you and your righteousness to those who are upright in heart.

Selected Bibliography

Adler, Cyrus and J. M. Casanowicz, "Arba' Kanfot." Pages 75–76 in vol. 2 of *The Jewish Encyclopedia*. Edited by Isidore Singer and Cyrus Adler. 12 vols. London: Funk & Wagnalls Company, 1902.

Bivin, David. "The Hem of His Garment." *Jerusalem Perspective* 7 (1988), 2.

Bivin, David. *New Light on the Difficult Words of Jesus: Insights from His Jewish Context*. Holland, MI: En Gedi Resource Center, 2005.

Chavel, Charles B. *Maimonides: The Commandments*. 2 vols. New York: Soncino Press, 1967.

Cohen, Rabbi Alfred ed. *Tekhelet: The Renaissance of a Mitzvah*. Hoboken, NJ; KTAV, 1996.

Gandz, Solomon. "The Knot in Hebrew Literature, or from the Knot to the Alphabet." *Isis* 14:1 (May 1930): 189–214.

Kaplan, Rabbi Aryeh. *Tzitzith: A Thread of Light*. New York: National Conference of Synagogue Youth, 1991.

Kirshenbaum, Aaron. "Concerning the Threads of Zizith." Pages 246–252 *Studies in Judaism: Jubilee Volume Presented to David Kotlar*. Edited by A. M. Rabello. Tel Aviv: Am Hasseffer, 1975 [Hebrew].

Maimonides, Moses. *Maimonides Mishneh Torah: Hilchot Tefillin UMezuzah V'Sefer Torah Hilchot Tzitzit*. Translated by Rabbi Eliyahu Touger; Jerusalem: Moznaim Publishing, 1988.

Milgrom, Jacob. "Of Hems and Tassels." *Biblical Archaeological Review* (May/June 1993): 61–65.

Stephens, Ferris J. "The Ancient Significance of Sîsîth." *Journal of Biblical Literature* 50:2 (1931): 59–70.

Weiner, Jason. "*Tzitzit*—In or Out?" *The Journal of Halacha and Contemporary Society* XLIX (Spring 2005): 105–121.

Endnotes

1   Paraphrased from Matthew 9:20–22; Mark 5:24–34; Luke 8:42–48.

2   Matthew 14:36; Mark 6:56.

3   Zechariah 8:23.

4   "One might think that these are two Commandments – the Commandment of the blue and the Commandment of the white; Scripture therefore states, *And it shall be unto you for a fringe* [Numbers 15:39], thus showing it is one Commandment and not two" (*Sifre* 115). See Charles B. Chavel, *Maimonides the Commandments* (2 vols.; New York: Soncino Press, 1967), 1:22.

5   Ibid., 1:22.

6   Scholars suggest that it is related to the Babylonian *sisiktu* and Sumerian *TÚG.SÍG.* See Ferris J. Stephens, "The Ancient Significance of Sîsîth," *Journal of Biblical Literature* 50:2 (1931), 59–70.

7   Jeffery Tigay, *The JPS Torah Commentary: Deuteronomy* (New York: The Jewish Publication Society, 1996), 203. *Gedilim* comes from the root word *gadal* (גדל) meaning to "bind or twist together." It is also related to the Aramaic (גדילא) "plaited locks."

8   *Sifre* 115.

9   Milgrom, *The JPS Torah Commentary*, 410. Also Aaron Kirshenbaum, "Concerning the Threads of Zizith," *Studies in Judaism: Jubilee Volume Presented to David Koltar* (Tel Aviv: Am Hasseffer, 1975), 246-252 [Hebrew].

10   Milgrom, *The JPS Torah Commentary*, 410.

11   Kirshenbaum, "Concerning the Threads of Zizith," 246-252.

12   Stephens, "The Ancient Significance of Sîsîth," 59–70.

13   Jacob Milgrom, "Of Hems and Tassels," *Biblical Archaeological Review* May/June (1993), 61–65.

14   Stephens, "The Ancient Significance of Sîsîth," 59–70.

15   Ibid., 59–70.

16 Milgrom, *The JPS Torah Commentary*, 410–411.

17 E. A. Speiser, "*Palil* and Congeners: A Sampling of Apotropaic Symbols," *Assyriological Studies* 16 (April 21, 1965), 389–393.

18 Speiser, "*Palil* and Congeners," 393.

19 Alexander Scheiber, *The Role of Tzitzit in Agreements* (Budapest: P. Hirschler Memorial Book, 1949). See there for an entire discussion of this practice.

20 It should be noted that according to Yadin the women's garments had "gamma-shaped pattern" in contrast to the men's who had stripes. See Yadin, *The Finds from the Bar Kokhba Period in the cave of Letters* (Jerusalem: The Israel Exploration society, 1963), 227–232.

21 Douglas Edwards, "Dress and Ornamentation," *Anchor Bible Dictionary* 2:232–38. See also Benjamin Mazar, ed., *Views of the Biblical World* (5 volumes; Jerusalem: International Publishing Co., 1960), 3:212–213.

22 Also see t.*Tohorot* 8:13 and m.*Meilah* 5:1.

23 See Marcus Jastrow, "חלוק," *A Dictionary of the Targumim, the Talmud Babli and Yerushalmi, and the Midrashic Literature* (2 vols.; New York: Pardes Publishing House, 1950), 1:465. Although in the Septuagint the more likely corresponding term is *kutonet* (כתנת), by the time of the Master it was most likely called a *chaluk*. David Bivin, "The Hem of His Garment," *Jerusalem Perspective* 7 (1988), 2. Yadin notes that the *chaluk* was usually made of two separate pieces of cloth which is why there is special mention of the Master's one-piece tunic in John 19:23-24. Yigdal Yadin, *Bar-Kokhba: The Rediscovery of the Legendary Hero of the Second Temple Jewish Revolt Against Rome*, (New York: Random House, 1971), 69.

24 Bivin, "The Hem of His Garment," 2. In the Septuagint the more likely corresponding term is *beged* (בגד), but by the time of the Master it was most likely called a *tallit*. See also Jastrow, "טלית," *A Dictionary of the Targumim, the Talmud Babli and Yerushalmi, and the Midrashic Literature*, 1:537. Franz Delitzsch also uses *tallit* in his Hebrew rendering of the Greek New Testament. The tallit could also be made of linen, see b.*Menachot* 39b.

25 Marie-Henriette Gates, "Dura-Europas: A Fortress of Syro Mesopotamian Art" *The Biblical Archaeologist* 47:3 (September 1984): 175.

26 Bivin, "The Hem of His Garment," 2.

27 See b.*Shabbat* 147a, b.*Menachot* 41a, and b.*Rosh HaShannah* 17b.

28 b.*Bava Batra* 57b.

29 "Tallit," *Encyclopedia Judaica 2nd Edition* 19:465.

30   Ibid. "Anyone who is not a scholar, and parades in the scholar's cloak, is not admitted within the circle of the Holy One, blessed be He" (b.*Bava Batra* 98a).

31   Rabbi Abraham Ibn Ezra, *Ibn Ezra's Commentary on the Torah: Numbers* (trans. H. Norman Strickman and Arthur M. Silver; New York: Menorah Publishing Company, 1999), 124.

32   See Rabbi Moses ben Maimon, *Maimonides Mishneh Torah: Hilchot Tefillin UMezuzah V'Sefer Torah Hilchot Tzitzit* (trans. Rabbi Eliyahu Touger; Jerusalem: Moznaim Publishing, 1988), 234.

33   Cyrus Adler and J. M. Casanowicz, "Arba' Kanfot," *Jewish Encyclopedia* 2:75–76.

34   Yadin, *The Finds from the Bar Kokhba Period*, 186, 219–240.

35   Yadin, *Bar-Kokhba*, 73. These stripes help identify what was a man's garment and what was a woman's garment. The woman's garments had an "L-like" pattern at the four corners.

36   With regard to the linen, it was not dyed, as it did not take. The people of Israel considered linen attractive because it was naturally white, without dyeing. See Kirshenbaum, "Concerning the Threads of Zizith," 246-252 [Hebrew] and Yadin, *The Finds from the Bar Kokhba Period*, 186–187.

37   Ibid., 186.

38   See Leviticus 9:19 and Deuteronomy 22:11.

39   b.*Menachot* 39b. This requirement was due to the juxtaposition of the commandment of tzitzit in Deuteronomy to that of the prohibition of mixing wool and linen. It was read in the sense of one should not mix wool and linen except in tzitzit. Cf. *Leviticus Rabbah* 22:10.

40   Yosef Tobi, "Challenges to Tradition: Jewish Cultures in Yemen, Iraq, Iran, Afghanistan, and Burkhara," in *Cultures of the Jews: A New History* (ed. David Biale; New York: Schocken Books, 2002), 938.

41   Tobi, "Challenges to Tradition," 945.

42   Outside influence from the greater Jewish community was brought in during the Ottoman occupation (1536–1635) and was "strengthened" in the 1730s with new leadership, but was really not felt heavily until the first half of the twentieth century. See Yoseph Tobi, *The Jews of Yemen: Studies in their History and Culture*, (Boston: Brill, 1999), 208–209.

43   See Tobi, *The Jews of Yemen*, 209.

44   Rav Yosef Kafah, *Halikhot Teman* (Jerusalem: Mahad, 2002), 22–23 n. 6. Translation taken and modified from Rav Yosph QafaH, "Halichoth Teman: Preparing for Shabboth," n.p. [cited 24 March 2011] Online: http://www.chayas.com/homeschoolsabbath.htm.

45   See Rav Yosef Kafah's edition of Rambam's *Mishneh Torah*, 1:6:13.

46   Taken from Dr. Aaron Gimani, "The Source of a Custom," n.p. [cited 5 November 2008]. Online: http://www.biu.ac.il/JH/Parasha/eng/shelach/gimani.htm. See b.*Taanit* 23a for a Talmudic example of carrying wood on a tallit.

47   "The sages of Yemen employed the corner of the tallit to make a *kinyan sudar* (a form of contractual agreement whereby the seller or buyer lifts up an object—often a handkerchief—which the other gives him). Rabbi Y. Kafich, esteemed Yemenite Rabbi and scholar, considers this use of the tallit a tradition of ancient times, and this receives some support from Saadia Gaon, for in his commentary on the book of Proverbs, Saadia compares "You have struck your hands for a stranger" (Prov. 6:1) to the procedure for a kinyan, remarking that the best garment for this purpose is one that reminds us of the mitzvot (commandments). The Yemenite practice of using a corner of a tallit for a kinyan sudar is therefore most appropriate, since we are told in Numbers 15:39 that looking at the tzitziyot should make us 'remember all the commandments of the Lord.'" See Gimani, "The Source of a Custom," n.p.

48   b.*Menachot* 39a. While some authorities argue that this is only for tzitzit with *techelet*, Rambam argues that this is valid even without *techelet*. See *Mishneh Torah, Hilchot Tzitzit* 1:9.

49   See Rav Yosef Kafah's edition of Rambam's *Mishneh Torah*, 2:20.

50   Rabbi Yitshak ben Nisim Ratsabi, *Olat Yitshak: Zeh Sefer Imre Shefer Sheelot u'Teshuvot* (2 vols.; Benei Brak: Maharits, 1989): 2:31–32 (Hebrew). Translation from Gimani, "The Source of the Custom," n.p.

51   See parallels in Mark 5:25–34 and Luke 8:43–48. Also Matthew 14:36 and Mark 6:56.

52   David Bivin, *New Light on the Difficult Words of Jesus: Insights from His Jewish Context* (Holland, MI: En Gedi Resource Center, 2005), 49.

53   See b.*Sotah* 22a. Jodi Magnes writes: "The Synoptic Gospels suggest that Jesus belonged to a minority of Jews who wore the fringed mantle, for it is hard to imagine why the gospel writers would have fabricated a detail of clothing that was unfamiliar to most non-Jewish readers and reflected a strict observance of Jewish law by Jesus" (Jodi Magnes, *Stone and Dung, Oil and Spit: Jewish Daily Life in the Time of Jesus* (Grand Rapids, MI: Eerdmans, 2011), 118.

54   Taken from David Bivin, "The New International Jesus," *Jerusalem Perspective* 56 (September/November 1999): 20–24. Bivin has a list of seven translations that do this in the article.

55   The tzitzit may have been tied in a similar fashion to that of the *Temanim*.

56 J. Derrett writes, "Men and women kept the head covered in prayer (we must leave aside the practice during mourning, as irrelevant) until (as is evident) the church broke away from the synagogue, and, on doctrinal grounds, took up the custom (which the Greeks would welcome) of praying bareheaded: that is to say, the males did." See J. Duncan M. Derrett, "Religious Hair," in *Studies in the New Testament* (6 volumes; Leiden, Brill: 1977), 1:171. Also note in 1 Kings 19:13 Elijah's outer garment is big enough to cover his head with it; *Leviticus Rabbah* 23:6; and a story about Nakdimon ben Gorion in *Avot DeRabbi Natan* 6.

57 Yigael Yadin, *The Finds from the Bar Kokhba Period*, 223.

58 Samuel Tobias Lachs, *A Rabbinic Commentary of the New Testament* (Hoboken, NJ: KTAV Publishing House, 1987), 172. See also Lachs article "The End of the Blue Thread," in *Jewish Civilization: Essays and Studies* (ed. Ronald A. Brauner; 2 vols.; Philadelphia: Reconstructionist Rabbinical College, 1981), 2:5–61 where he notes other cultures that have similar sentiments about knotted strings.

59 It is of interest to note that both Channan the Hidden and Choni the Circle-Drawer come from the same spiritual tradition of charismatic wonder-working *chasidim* that many scholars believe the Master fits well into. See Shmuel Safrai, "Jesus and the Hasidim," *Jerusalem Perspective* 42–44 (January–June 1994), 3–22 and Geza Vermes, *Jesus the Jew* (Philadelphia: Fortress Press, 1981), 58–82.

60 See also Mark 12:38 and Luke 20:46 where the Master criticizes the length of the *tallit*. Perhaps they are lengthening beyond the norm found in b.*Bava Batra* 57b.

61 "For the elders of the House of Shammai and the elders of the house of Hillel gathered in the upper room and said, 'There is no fixed measure to the length of the fringe'" (*Sifre* 115). See Jacob Neusner, *Sifré to Numbers: An American Translation and Explanation Volume Two Sifré to Numbers 59–115* (Atlanta: Scholars Press: 1986), 176.

62 S. Safrai and M. Stern, eds., *The Jewish People in the First Century: Historical Geography, Political History, Social, Cultural and religious Life and Institutions* (2 vols.; Philadelphia, PA: Fortress Press, 1987), 2:798.

63 b.*Gittin* 56a.

64 It must be remembered though that the tallit of those days extended well below the knees so that for the tzitzit to touch the ground they would not have to be very long. Today it is halachically forbidden to let one's tzitzit's drag on the floor as according to the *Mishnah Berurah* it is "contempt for the mitzvah." See *Mishnah Berurah, Orach Chayim* 22:18.

65 Nahum Sarna, *The JPS Torah Commentary: Exodus* (Philadelphia: The Jewish Publication Society, 1991), 13.

66 b.*Menachoth* 43b.

67 Milgrom, *The JPS Torah Commentary: Numbers*, 127.

68 Solomon Gandz, "The Knot in Hebrew Literature, or from the Knot to the Alphabet," *Isis* 14:1 (May, 1930), 189–214.

69 Rabbi Uziel Milevsky, *Ner Uziel: Perspectives on the Parashah* (2 vol.; Southfield, MI: Targum Press, 2002), 2:176.

70 Paul P. Levertoff, *Midrash Sifre on Numbers* (London: A. Golub, 1926), 107.

71 Jacob Immanuel Schochet, *Tzava'at Harivash: The Testimony of Rabbi Israel Baal Shem Tov* (Brooklyn, NY: Kehot, 1998), 18.

72 *Zohar* III, 175a.

73 Translation from Rabbi Chaim Miller, *Chumash: The Book of Numbers* (Brooklyn: Kol Menachem, 2005), 127.

74 Rabbi Samson Raphael Hirsch, *The Pentateuch: Numbers* (trans. Isaac Levy; Gateshead: Judaica Press, 1999), 262–263.

75 Rabbi Hirsch, *The Pentateuch*, 263.

76 See Exodus 26:1, 4, 31, 36, and 27:16.

77 See Leviticus 19:19 and Deuteronomy 22:11.

78 Sarna, *The JPS Torah Commentary: Exodus*, 156.

79 For the suggestion that the Essenes had linen *techelet* see Magnes, *Stone and Dung, Oil and Spit: Jewish Daily Life in the Time of Jesus*, 111–117.

80 b.*Menachot* 39b; cf. Leviticus Rabbah 22:10. For a critical study on this passage and an inquiry into whether or not the Essenes ascribed to this tradition, see Magnes, *Stone and Dung, Oil and Spit: Jewish Daily Life in the Time of Jesus*, 111–117.

81 b.*Yevamot* 4b.

82 See Rashi to Deuteronomy 22:12.

83 Jacob Milgrom, "Of Hems and Tassels," *Biblical Archaeological Review* May/June (1993), 61–65.

84 Yadin, *The Finds from the Bar Kokhba Period*, 186–187. Additionally "no linen mantles were found in the cave," i.e., the linen parts were not for linen garments.

85 John Joseph Owen, *Analytical Key to the Old Testament* (4 vols.; Grand Rapids: Baker Book House, 1999), 849.

86 Translation from Paul P. Levertoff, *Midrash Sifre on Numbers* (London: A. Golub, 1926), 109.

87 Rabbi Aryeh Kaplan, *Tzitzith: A Thread of Light* (New York: National Conference of Synagogue Youth, 1991), 4.

88 Rabbi Uziel Milevsky, *Ner Uziel*, 176.

89 Compare the Jewish-Christian document *Recognitions of Clement* 4:9 (Coxe): "When God had made man after His own image and likeness, He grafted into His work a certain breathing and odour of His divinity, that so men, being made partakers of His Only-begotten, might through Him be also friends of God and sons of adoption."

90 Rabbi Yosef Yitchak Schneerson, *HaYom Yom* (Brooklyn, NY: Kehot, 2005), 112.

91 *Likutey Halakhoth*, *Genevah* 5:15 Translation from Rabbi Nachman of Breslov, *Rabbi Nachman's Stories* (trans. Rabbi Aryeh Kaplan; New York: The Breslov Research Institute, 1983), 107.

92 Rabbi Menachem Mendel of Lubavitch, *Derech Mitzvosecha: A Mystical Perspective on the Commandments* (trans. Rabbi Eliyahu Touger; New York: Sichos in English, 2004), 406–407.

93 Translated from Yitzhak Buxbaum, *Jewish Spiritual Practices* (Northvale, New Jersey: Jason Aronson, 1990), 105–106.

94 Translated from Ibid., 106.

95 *Zohar* III:260a.

96 Translation from Rev. A. M'Caul, *Rabbi David Kimchi's Commentary Upon the Prophecies of Zechariah Translated from Hebrew* (London, England: Macintosh Printer), 81.

97 For a good discussion of tucking one's tzitzit in or wearing them out see Jason Weiner, "*Tzitzit*—In or Out?" *The Journal of Halacha and Contemporary Society* XLIX (Spring 2005): 105–121.

98 *Sifre* 115.

99 Kaplan, *Tzitzith*, 12.

100 b.*Menachot* 39b; see Kaplan, *Tzitzith*, 12–13.

101 Kaplan, *Tzitzith*, 14.

102 b.*Menachot* 39a.

103 Kaplan, *Tzitzith*, 14.

104 b.*Menachot* 39a.

105 *Hilchot Tzitzit* 1:1. Translation from Rabbi Moses ben Maimon, *Maimonides Mishneh Torah:Hilchot Tefillin UMezuzah V'Sefer Torah Hilchot Tzitzit*,194.

106 *Shulchan Aruch HaRav, Orach Chayim* 24:9; *Mishnah Berurah* 9:5.

107 *Hilchot Tzitzit* 2:8. Translation from Rabbi Moses ben Maimon, *Maimonides Mishneh Torah:Hilchot Tefillin UMezuzah V'Sefer Torah Hilchot*, 216.

108 b.*Menachot* 38a.

109 Milgrom, *The JPS Torah Commentary: Numbers*, 128.

110 See Rabbi Moses ben Maimon, *Maimonides Mishneh Torah:Hilchot Tefillin UMezuzah V'Sefer Torah Hilchot Tzitzit*, 217 n.12.

111 *Shulchan Aruch HaRav, Orach Chayim* 24:9. It is acceptable to have a colored strip on the tallit, so long as the majority of it is white.

112 *Hilchot Tzitzit* 1:11.

113 This is based on Rabbeinu Tam's interpretation of b.*Menachot* 39a, 41b. The Rambam interprets the same passage in the Talmud as requiring only four fingerbreaths. See Rabbi Moses ben Maimon, *Maimonides Mishneh Torah:Hilchot Tefillin UMezuzah V'Sefer Torah Hilchot Tzitzit*, 198.

114 b.*Menachot* 44a.

115 b.*Menachot* 40a.

116 b.*Menachot* 38b.

117 Milgrom, *The JPS Torah Commentary: Numbers* (New York: The Jewish Publication Society, 1990), 412.

118 Jonah Mandel, "The Color 'Techelet,'" n.p. [cited 13 April 2011]. Online: http://www.jpost.com/JewishWorld/JewishNews/Article.aspx?id=210753. For an in-depth study of the resurgence of *techelet*, see Rabbi Alfred Cohen, ed., *Tekhelet: The Renaissance of a Mitzvah* (Hoboken, NJ; KTAV, 1996).

119 The minor opinion states that two should be dyed with *techelet*.

120 Rabbi Moses ben Maimon, *Maimonides Mishneh Torah:Hilchot Tefillin UMezuzah V'Sefer Torah Hilchot Tzitzit*, 199.

121 Ibid., 199.

122 b.*Menachot* 43b; *Hilchot Tzitzit* 3:1.

123 Kaplan, *Tzitzith*, 28.

124 E.g., *Mishnah Berurah* 10:37. The minimum size is the same as the *tallit katan*, one amah (cubit) squared. See Kaplan, *Tzitzith*, 32.

125 See also *Hilchot Tzitzit* 2:7 and *Mishnah Berurah* 20:1.

126 *Mishnah Berurah* 20:2.

127 As non-Jewish servants to Jews they would only be required to perform the same mitzvot as Jewish women.

128 Translation from Rabbi Moses Maimonides, *Maimonides Mishneh Torah: Sefer Shoftim* (trans. Rabbi Eliyahu Touger; Jerusalem, Israel: Moznaim Publishing, 1988), 604.

129 In *Hilchot Melachim* 10:9 the Rambam does prohibit a Gentile from Shabbat and Torah study.

130 *Shoneh Halachot, Siman* 304. This is also the opinion of the Chatam Sofer (Commentary to *b.Cullin* 33a).

131 While the rabbis never really come right out and say that Gentiles are not permitted to wear tzitzit, there are a few other prohibitions associated with non-Jews and tzitzit. For example, most halachahic authorizes agree that a Gentile is not permitted to make tzitzit for a Jew based on the injunction "Speak to the sons of Israel." See *Mishnah Berurah* 14:1. Cf. *Mishnah Berurah* 11:2, 21:3, 21:16–17.

132 Sometimes tzitzit are listed in *mitzvot* forbidden to Noachides, but there is not a specific halachic source to base this on.

133 *Responsa Egrot Moshe, Yore Deah* 2:7. Others such as Rabbi Yoel Schwartz say it is permissible but that they must be tied in such as way that does not confuse them with Jewish ones. See *Service from the Heart* (ed. Rabbi Michael Katzet al.; Rose, OK: Oklahoma B'nai Noah Society, 2007), 303.

134 E.g., Romans 11; Ephesians 2:12–13.